TO:

FROM:

PuRR

For every cat in the world.
We would be lost without you.

Designed by Kathy Weller

Published by Peter Pauper Press, Inc.
202 Mamaroneck Avenue
White Plains, NY 10601

ISBN 978-1-4413-1749-0
Printed in China
7 6 5 4 3
Visit us at www.peterpauper.com

KITTY
YOGA

HAVE YOU EVER WONDERED WHAT YOUR CAT IS THINKING?

THE ANCIENT AND ARCANE TRUTHS OF THE INNER WORLD OF DOMESTIC FELINES ARE NOW FINALLY EXPLAINED WITH

KITTY YOGA

..WHY DOES SHE DO THE THINGS SHE DOES?

MEDITATE ON THE AGE-OLD WISDOM INHERENT IN EACH KITTY YOGA POSE, AND ENJOY A DEEPER UNDERSTANDING OF YOUR FURRY FRIEND THAN EVER BEFORE.

NAMASTE.

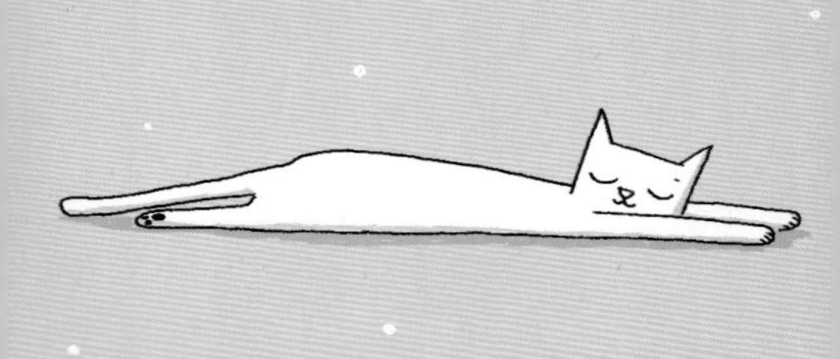

FOUNDATION POSES

MOUNTAIN POSE

MOUNTAIN POSE IS THE
STRONG FOUNDATION OF MANY
KITTY YOGA POSES. IT IS
THE FIRST STEP ON THE PATH
TO KITTY YOGA ENLIGHTENMENT.

• • •

THE PEACEFULNESS YOU EXUDE
IN THIS POSE WILL ENCOURAGE
THOSE AROUND YOU TO BE
OPEN-MINDED AND TRUSTING.

• • •

THIS IN TURN WILL HELP YOU
TO REACH THE STATE OF NIRVANA
BY THE FULFILLMENT OF YOUR
HIGHER NEEDS THROUGH THE
GENEROSITY OF THE UNQUESTIONING
SOULS SURROUNDING YOU.

NAMASTE.

EASY POSE

RELAX ON BELLY,
LEGS EXTENDED.

INHALE.

EXHALE.

PURR.

DON'T MOVE FROM THIS POSE
UNLESS YOU ARE FORCED TO.

NAMASTE.

CORPSE POSE

• • •

LIE ON BACK.

CLOSE EYES. RELAX LIMBS.

FEEL ALL TENSION MELT AWAY.

EMBRACE YOUR FULL
LAZINESS WITH GRATITUDE.
PURR.

MEDITATE INDEFINITELY.

NAMASTE.

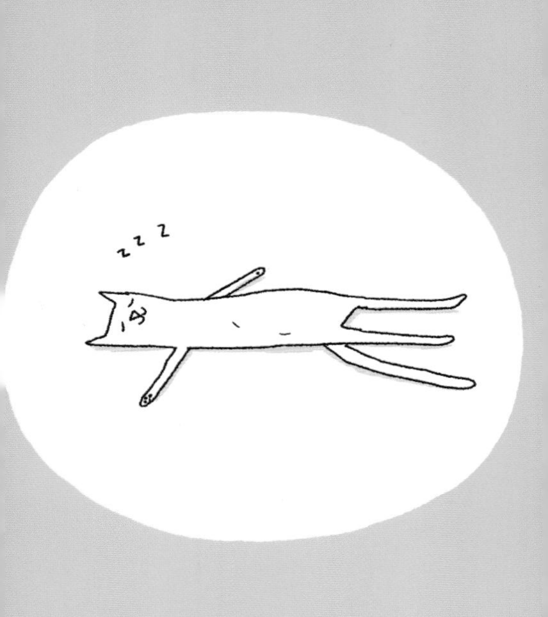
z z Z

ACTIVE POSES

LORD OF THE DANCE POSE

PROP: YOGA (LITTER) BOX

BEGIN IN MOUNTAIN POSE.
STAND UPRIGHT AND STEP INTO
YOGA BOX, ONE LIMB AT A TIME.
BREATHE.

EXHALE.
INHALE.
EXHALE.

ONCE ENSCONCED, LIFT PAWS IN
PATTERN – ALTERNATING RIGHT AND
LEFT, FRONT AND BACK – FLICKING
PAWS BACKWARD WHILE KICKING
BAD KARMA AWAY FROM YOU.

{ THIS WILL MATERIALIZE IN
THE FORM OF KITTY LITTER. }

EAGLE POSE

PROP: MOUSE

REST HIGH ON STAIR PEAK,
IN MOUNTAIN POSE.

• • •

FOCUS ON MOUSE CHAKRA BELOW.

• • •

LEAP OVER CHAKRA AND DESCEND,
IN A WEIGHTLESS, FLOWING
MOVEMENT, LIKE A BEAUTIFUL
BIRD IN FLIGHT.

• • •

LAND SPREAD-EAGLED.

• • •

FEEL MOUSE CHAKRA
ENERGY SCURRY AWAY.

• • •

NOTE: AFTER PRACTICING
THIS ADVANCED POSE,
AN ICE PACK MAY BE NECESSARY.

CAT POSE

CAT POSE OFTEN OCCURS INSTINCTIVELY AS A PHYSIOLOGICAL RESPONSE TO NATURALLY OCCURING PHENOMENA, SUCH AS A VACUUM CLEANER.

CAT POSE CAN ALSO BE PRACTICED FOR SPIRITUAL AND CHAKRA-BALANCING BENEFIT.

• • •

STANDING ON ALL FOURS, ARCH BACK TOWARD THE SKY.

INHALE (LOUD NOISE ANNOYANCE). EXHALE (COURAGE AND PEACE).

CONTINUE BREATHING EXERCISE UNTIL COMPLETE AND TOTAL RELAXATION PERMEATES YOU.

OR VACUUM STOPS RUNNING. WHICHEVER COMES FIRST.

CHAIR POSE

PROPS: CHAIR, DOG

DEFTLY SNEAK UNDER SEATING OCCUPIED BY ANNOYING DOG.

• • •

STRETCH FORELEG OVERHEAD, UTILIZING DOG TAIL AS A FLEXIBILITY METER.

• • •

BAT DOG'S TAIL FIRMLY BUT GENTLY WITH PAW. CONTINUE ACTIVE POSE UNTIL DOG VACATES SEATING, LEAVING IT FREE FOR YOU.

GARLAND POSE

PROP: STRING OF LIGHTS

A GARLAND OF LIGHT ENERGY
HAS A MYSTICAL, MAGNETIC AURA
THAT DRAWS KITTY IN
LIKE A MOTH TO A FLAME.

• • •

THIS FREE-FORM POSE ENCOURAGES
SPIRITED CIRCULAR MOVEMENT,
CENTERING KITTY CHI.

• • •

WHEN BALANCE WANES,
DROP TO GROUND INTO EASY POSE,
AND EMBRACE GARLAND
WITH UNIVERSAL LOVE AND LIGHT.

• • •

AFTER LONG MEDITATION, DETANGLE.

UPWARD DOG POSE

PROP: DOG

LIE ON GROUND, FACING DOG.

INHALE.

EXHALE WITH GROWLING UJJAYI BREATH.

FOCUS INTENTION ON DOG.

WITH ACTIVE ENERGY AND
STRONG LEGS, HOP ON DOG'S HEAD.

EMBRACE HEAD WITH
POWERFUL UNIVERSAL LOVE.

DOG WILL RESPOND PHYSICALLY,
JUMPING UP AND RUNNING AWAY
TO SPREAD THE POSITIVE ENERGY
YOU STIRRED INSIDE HIM.

PROP: HUMAN

SUPPORTED HEADSTAND POSE

BEGIN IN MOUNTAIN POSE
ON HUMAN LAP.

INHALE AND EXHALE WITH A FULL
BODY STRETCH, SCALING
ARMS AND SHOULDERS OF HUMAN.

• • •

CONTINUE TO CLIMB UP,
GENTLY FINDING BALANCE
AS YOU GO.

• • •

WHEN STEADINESS IS ACHIEVED
UPON HUMAN CROWN CHAKRA,
PRACTICE RHYTHMIC YOGA BREATHING.

HOLD POSE INDEFINITELY
(OR UNTIL HUMAN DISPERSES YOUR CHI.)

HIGH LUNGE POSE

PROP: BOOKCASE

BEGIN IN MOUNTAIN POSE
FACING BOOKCASE.

• • •

INHALE AND EXHALE TO
PREPARE FOR ANAEROBIC BURST.

• • •

LUNGE UP, PUSHING STRONGLY
OFF HIND LEGS, AND STRETCH
SPINE WITH STRONG FORELIMBS
TO CONNECT TO SHELF.

• • •

GRIP WITH STABILIZER MUSCLES
AND PULL UP, USING SPINAL ENERGY.

• • •

WHEN LANDING IS ACHIEVED,
TIGHTLY CURL UP INTO
INNER SHELF CORNER TO
COUNTERBALANCE ROCKING BOOKCASE.

{ NAMASTE. }

BOW POSE

PROPS: CURTAINS, CURTAIN RODS

BOW POSE IS AN ADVANCED-LEVEL POSE THAT REQUIRES STRENGTH AND STAMINA. IRONICALLY, IT IS ONLY ACHIEVED AS A RESULT OF A MISCALCULATED JUMP.

BEGIN IN MOUNTAIN POSE. ASCEND CURTAINS, USING CLIMBING TECHNIQUES FROM HIGH LUNGE POSE. WHEN SUMMIT IS REACHED, SCALE CURTAIN ROD. LEAP TO NEIGHBORING ROD.

WHEN ATTEMPT FALLS SHORT, BOW POSE IS ACCOMPLISHED!

BASK IN THE GLORY OF ACHIEVING THIS CHALLENGING POSITION!

TO COMPLETE POSE, MEOW LOUDLY TO ATTRACT HUMAN RESCUE (OR DOG TO FALL ON).

UPWARD PLANK POSE

APPROACH THE PLANK.
USING A RHYTHMIC MOTION,
SLINK SIDEWAYS, SIDESWIPING
PLANK WITH STEADY PRESSURE.

• • •

BEGIN AT WHISKER AND SLIDE
THROUGH TO LOWER TRUNK.

• • •

WHEN SEQUENCE IS COMPLETE,
TURN AROUND AND REPEAT ON OTHER
SIDE. REMEMBER TO BREATHE.

REPEAT SEQUENCE UNTIL URGE TO
ATTACK HUMAN HAND SURFACES.

PROP: UPWARD PLANK
(EXAMPLES: HUMAN LEG,
CHAIR LEG, OR EDGE OF TABLE)

PROP: ECONOMY-SIZE KIBBLE

COWFACE POSE

HOP WITH WEIGHTLESS GRACE
INTO BAG OF KITTY KIBBLE.

• • •

LAND SOFT AND STILL.

• • •

ABSORB NOURISHING ENERGY
IN CRUNCHING MEDITATION.

• • •

WHEN FULLNESS CHAKRA
IS ENERGIZED, GENTLY SLIDE
OUT OF BAG AND ONTO FLOOR.

• • •

SETTLE INTO CORPSE POSE.

SANTOSHA.

OUTDOOR POSES

PROPS: TREE, NEST, BIRD

TREE POSE

ASCEND TREE IN
AN ACTIVE STRETCH.

• • •

BREATHE,
KEEPING HEART CHAKRA OPEN.
THIS WILL ASSIST BIRD CHI
IN ACCEPTING KITTY KARMA.

• • •

SLOWLY CLIMB AND BALANCE
TO BECOME LEVEL
WITH NEST OF BIRD.

• • •

WHEN NEST IS REACHED,
BIRD CHI WILL ENGAGE
IN SPIRITED SONG
AND ENERGETIC DANCE.

COBRA POSE

PROPS: SHRUB, CATNIP

TIP: TO MASTER COBRA, ONE MUST UTILIZE "SLITHERING," A COMBINATION OF STRENGTH AND FLEXIBILITY WORK FOUND ONLY IN KITTY YOGA.

BEGIN IN MOUNTAIN POSE,
BEHIND SHRUB, FOR COVER.

• • •

SLITHER TOWARDS CATNIP, STAYING
WEIGHTLESS AND LOW TO THE GROUND.

• • •

BREATHE.

• • •

WHEN CATNIP IS ATTAINED, REACH PAWS
AROUND PLANTER IN DEEP EMBRACE.

• • •

ACTIVATE STRONG STRETCH AND
HOLD FOR SEVERAL DEEP BREATHS.

• • •

PLEASE NOTE: THIS POSE IS KNOWN
TO CAUSE "SPIRITEDNESS" IN EVEN
THE MOST RESERVED KITTY YOGIS.

FEATHERED PEACOCK POSE

PROP: BIRD

BEGIN IN MOUNTAIN POSE.

BE STILL.

OBSERVE EXTERNAL POINT
OF ACTIVE BIRD PRANA.

BE STILL.

INHALE. EXHALE. INHALE.

WHEN BIRD ENERGY LANDS ON HEAD,
QUICKLY RELOCATE BIRD
ENERGY TO SAFE, STRONG JAW.

RELEASE THE FEATHERY CHI
TO EXERCISE DHARMA.

(NO BIRD WAS HARMED IN
THE MAKING OF THIS BOOK.)

GATE POSE

FACE GATE IN MOUNTAIN POSE.
WITH BALANCED ENERGY,
LEAP STRONG AND HIGH,
STRETCHING LEGS AND
TORSO TO REACH.

• • •

COMPLETE CLIMB
WITH QUIET INTENTION.

• • •

WHEN GATE SUMMIT IS REACHED,
STUDY FLIGHT OF BEE
IN HARMONY WITH NATURE.

PROPS: GATE, BEE

THIS END UP

MULTI-POSE SEQUENCES

BOAT POSE

A "BOAT" IS A RARE, MYSTICAL GIFT BESTOWED ON KITTY YOGIS WHEN THEIR ENERGY NEEDS EXTRA BALANCING.

WHEN A BOAT IS DISCOVERED, IT IS OFTEN FILLED WITH ENERGY VIBRATION MOLECULES.

PROPS: "BOAT," ENERGY VIBRATION MOLECULES

JUMP INTO BOAT, STRETCH, PLAY, AND RELEASE TENSION INTO THE MOLECULES.

THE HIGHER THEY FLY AND THE FURTHER THEY FLOAT, THE HIGHER THE LEVEL OF KITTY CHAKRA CENTERING.

STAFF POSE

WHEN ENERGY VIBRATION
MOLECULES NEED RECHARGING,
HUMAN WILL MYSTICALLY APPEAR
TO CLEAR BOAT AWAY.

• • •

STAND SILENT AND TALL
AGAINST HIDDEN WALL,
SPINE LONG, LIKE A STAFF.
HOLD UNTIL HUMAN EXITS.

TIP: DO NOT RISK BEING SEEN BY
HUMAN, FOR THEY WILL DISRUPT
YOUR FRESHLY BALANCED ENERGY.

PROPS: "BOAT,"
ENERGY VIBRATION MOLECULES, HUMAN

DOWNWARD DOG POSE

QUIETLY BEGIN POSE
FROM DEEP LUNGE, BEHIND
LARGE, UNSUSPECTING DOG.

INHALE. EXHALE.

ACTIVATING BACK LEGS POWERFULLY,
PROPEL KITTY ZENERGY TOWARD DOG.
LAND CENTER ON DOG'S BACK.

• • •

GENTLY BUT WITH STEADY
STRENGTH, USE DEEP-CLAW FLEXING
TO ASSIST WITH BALANCE.

• • •

{ TIP: A SQUIRMING DOG WILL PROVIDE
AN ADDITIONAL BALANCE CHALLENGE. }

PROP: DOG

TRIANGLE POSE

PROP: FEATHER STICK

BEGIN IN MOUNTAIN POSE.
FOCUS DEEPLY ON
FEATHER STICK CHAKRA.

• • •

REACH HIGH, FORELEGS
OUTSTRETCHED, BODY LONG,
IN ATTEMPT TO COLLECT CHAKRA.

• • •

WHEN BALANCE GIVES WAY
TO GRAVITY, END POSE.

• • •

(OPTION: IF DOG IS HANDY,
TRANSITION TO DOWNWARD DOG.)

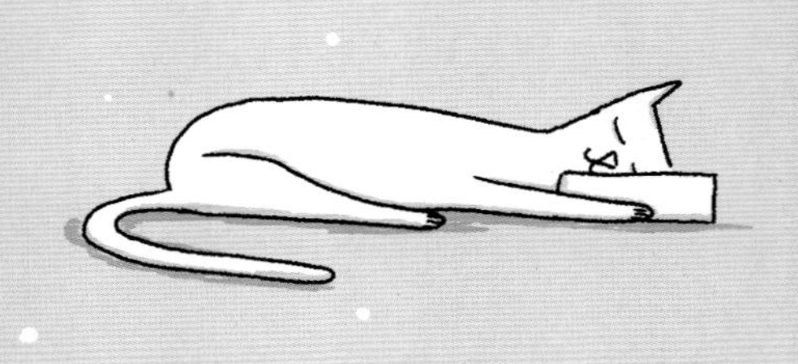

MEDITATION POSES

LION POSE

LIE STILL IN EASY POSE.

CLOSE EYES AND MEDITATE
ON YOUR OWN REGALITY
IN THE UNIVERSE.

THIS MENTAL STATE FUELS THE FUR CHAKRA TO EXPAND, OR 'FLUFF,' EVER SO SLOWLY.

WHEN FUR CHAKRA COMPLETES ITS FULL 'FLUFFING' CYCLE, PURRING MANTRA BEGINS AND LION POSE NIRVANA IS REACHED.

PIGEON POSE

PROPS: WINDOW, PIGEON

LIE RELAXED,
BEHIND GLASS WINDOW PANE.

QUIETLY OBSERVE PIGEON PRANA
ON THE OTHER SIDE OF THE WINDOW.

KNEAD WINDOW GLASS RHYTHMICALLY.

THIS POSE IS AN EXERCISE
IN MENTAL CONTROL OVER
KITTY'S PRIMAL URGES.
RELEASE THOSE INSTINCTS.
BE AT ONE WITH THE PIGEON.

• • •

NAMASTE.

NOOSE POSE

PROPS: CHAIR, DOG

BEGIN IN CHAIR ABOVE DOG.
SURVEY DOG POSITION.

• • •

ALLOW TAIL TO DESCEND
WEIGHTLESSLY UNDER DOG'S
CHIN, SLOWLY FLEXING
AROUND HIS NECK.

• • •

WHEN THE POSE IS SECURE,
PROCEED TO HOLD STRONG
FOR TEN BREATHS.
OR UNTIL DOG DEFENDS
HIMSELF. WHICHEVER
COMES FIRST.

FISH POSE

PROPS: CHAIR, FISH, BOWL

ON CHAIR IN MOUNTAIN POSE,
FACE FISH BOWL.
INHALE. EXHALE.

STRETCH FORWARD SLOWLY AND
METHODICALLY. MOVE CLOSER
TO FISH BOWL WITH EACH BREATH.

WHEN WHISKERS BRUSH BOWL,
FIND YOUR STILLNESS.

MEDITATE ON SWIMMING FISH
INTENSELY BUT PEACEFULLY.

USE THIS ZEN STATE TO
EXERCISE CONTROL OVER
YOUR PRIMAL KITTY IMPULSES.

OMMMM.

FIRE LOG POSE

PROP: LONG STRETCHY TUBE OF FABRIC
(SUCH AS HUMAN'S LONG-SLEEVE SHIRT)

BEGIN IN EASY POSE.
INHALE. EXHALE.

STRETCH FORWARD, USING FORELEGS AND PAWS TO OPEN TUBE.

MOVE THROUGH SLOWLY, HEAD FIRST, ALLOWING FABRIC TO HUG THE BODY AND MASSAGE THE FUR CHAKRA.

THIS MOVING MEDITATION WILL BUILD HEAT AND STATIC INSIDE THE SLEEVE, IMITATING THE WARMTH OF A CRACKLING FIRE.

CONTINUE TO ADVANCE THROUGH TINY TUBE UNTIL HEAD REACHES SMALL OPENING AT THE END.

DISENGAGE HEAD FROM HOLE.*
BREATHE.

* MEOW LOUDLY TO ATTRACT HUMAN ASSISTANCE FOR RELEASE FROM THIS POSE.

PROP: STRING

THREAD THE NEEDLE POSE

IN THIS POSE, STRING IS USED
AS A TOOL TO ENCOURAGE
FREE-FORM RELEASE OF
FRENETIC FELINE ENERGY
IN A SPIRITED MANNER.

OPTION: WHEN ENERGY PURGE
IS COMPLETE, MOVE INTO
COBRA POSE TO ATTAIN CATNIP
FOR A RESURGENCE OF FRESH ENERGY.

FALLEN WARRIOR POSE

PROPS: BOWL, MILK, KITCHEN FLOOR

SIT TALL IN MOUNTAIN POSE
FACING FULL BOWL
OF MILK ENERGY.

• • •

LAP UP ENTIRE BOWL WITH
INTENTION AND FOCUS.

• • •

WHEN BOWL IS EMPTY,
BREATHE DEEPLY. FALL INTO
MEDITATIVE STATE ON FLOOR,
HEADFIRST INTO BOWL.

• • •

SUBSIDE INTO ZEN-LIKE
PURR VIBRATION.

OM.

RECLINING BIG TOE POSE

BEGIN IN
MOUNTAIN POSE.

• • •

RECLINE AND EXTEND LEG
HIGH INTO AIR.
POINT TOES TOWARD SKY.

• • •

RELEASE TOES,
FLEX, AND REPEAT.

• • •

GROOMING WHILE IN
POSE IS OPTIONAL.

SPHINX POSE

PROP: DRIPPING FAUCET

SIT, RELAXED,
HEAD UNDER FAUCET.

• • •

ALLOW RHYTHMICALLY
FALLING DROPS OF WATER
TO MASSAGE SKULL
AND HYDRATE SOUL.

• • •

ALLOW STATE OF
MEDITATIVE ZEN
TO WASH OVER YOU.

• • •

OPTION: DRINK. BREATHE DEEPLY.
PERMIT YOGI WATER THERAPY
TO CLEANSE STATE OF MIND
AND QUENCH KITTY BODY.

PLANK POSE

PROP: CHAIR

LAY LOW AND BE SILENT
WHILE HUMAN PREPARES
TO VACATE PREMISES.

• • •

ONCE AREA IS CLEARED,
ASCEND BACK OF CHAIR,
UTILIZING FULL BODY STRETCH.
WORK CLAWS DEEP INTO FABRIC
OF CHAIR WITH EACH MOVEMENT.

• • •

WHEN SUMMIT IS SCALED,
DRAPE BODY LONG AND FLAT
ACROSS TOP OF CHAIR.

• • •

HOLD POSE FOR EIGHT HOURS,
OR UNTIL HUMAN RETURNS.

• • •

TIP: UPON HUMAN RETURN, VACATE
CHAIR TO AVOID HUMAN DISCOVERY OF
SCRATCHES AND KITTY YOGI FUZZ.

HALF MOON POSE

KITTY'S FINAL RELAXATION POSTURE

RECLINE AND ROLL BODY INTO NATURAL CRESCENT SHAPE.

BREATHE DEEPLY.

PURRING ENHANCES RELAXATION.

FOR ADDITIONAL PASSIVE STRETCH, HUG TAIL.

MEOW

NAMASTE

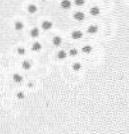

OMMM

MEOW
NAMASTE
OMMM
PURR